GOSPEL-CENTRED WORK

Becoming the worker God wants you to be

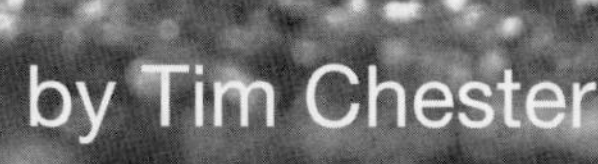

Gospel-Centred Work

The Good Book Company
Blenheim House, 1 Blenheim Road, Epsom, Surrey KT19 9AP, UK
Tel: 0333-123-0880; **International:** +44 (0) 208 942 0880
Email: admin@thegoodbook.co.uk

The Good Book Company (USA)
170 W. Main St, Purcellville VA, 20132
Tel: 866 244 2165; International: +1 866 244 2165
Email: sales@thegoodbook.com

Websites:
UK: www.thegoodbook.co.uk
North America: www.thegoodbook.com
Australia: www.thegoodbook.com.au
New Zealand: www.thegoodbook.co.nz

thegoodbook COMPANY

ISBN: 9781908762368

Cover design: André Parker
Printed in Singapore

CONTENTS

INTRODUCTION

Work is a big feature of the lives of most of us. Many go off to the factory, workshop, shop, office or classroom each morning. Others are at home looking after the house or children. An increasing number of people have a number of part-time jobs or work shifts.

Most people in full-time employment work about 40 hours a week. Some work much longer. That's at least a third of our waking hours. And when you add in the other work we do, like household chores, then we probably spend more than half our time working. We certainly spend more time working than on any other activity. Work is a big deal in our lives.

That means that if we want to be gospel-centred people living gospel-centred lives then we need to think through what gospel-centred work involves. What does it mean to live for Jesus in the workplace?

We need to connect Sunday morning and Monday morning. On Sunday morning we sing about God's love and power. But what does it mean to live in the light of God's love and power in an often hostile and pressured workplace? Is the person who sings God's praises on Sunday the same person on Monday when they face a difficult problem or an awkward customer or colleague?

That's what this book is about: a gospel-centred approach to the world of work. You can read it on your own. The short chapters mean you could readily read a chapter each morning on the commute to work. Or you could read it as part of a small group—perhaps a home group or a work-based fellowship. The Bible studies and discussion questions offer something for you to discuss together.

Finding your way around

Consider this

A scenario—often based on a real-life situation—which raises some kind of dilemma or frustration in our working lives.

Biblical background

A relevant Bible passage together with some questions to help you think it through.

Read all about it

A discussion of the principle, both in terms of its theological underpinning and its contemporary application.

Questions for reflection

Questions that can be used for group discussion or personal reflection.

Ideas for action

Some ideas or an exercise to help people think through the application of the principle to their own situation.

We have tried to make this book work:

- whether it is read by an individual or used as the basis for group discussion.
- whether you want to work through it systematically or turn to particular topics as they arise in your working life.

PART ONE

GOSPEL WORK

1 GOD WORKS

Principle

Expect work to be fun, fulfilling and exciting.

Consider this

Mark looked up at the clock. 4.55. Five minutes to go. Surely it wouldn't matter if they closed a minute or two early tonight. He looked at the pile of shoe boxes in the corner. They could wait till the morning. A few of the racks needed straightening. But they would only get untidy again. No, he was done for the day. He turned over the sign in the window—"closed"—and grabbed his coat.

Mandy looked up at the clock. 4.55. Five minutes to go. Another call came through. "Hello, how can I help you?" she said in her polite voice. Meanwhile she rolled her eyes at Christine and acted a yawn. "I'm afraid that's the best I can do", she said a few moments later. Then, once the call was over, she added for Christine's benefit, "... at 5pm after a long day".

By 7.20 Mark and Mandy were sitting in John's living room waiting for the rest of the house group to arrive. "How was work today?" John asked. They both sighed. "Same as always," grumbled Mandy. "It pays the bills", said Mark, before launching into a story about an annoying customer. John sat there listening, and wondered whether he should say anything about their attitude...

Biblical background

Read Genesis 1 v 1 – 2 v 2

- What similarities are there between God's work and our work?
- How does God view His work and His workmanship?
- What roles does God give to humanity?

Read all about it

God saw all that he had made, and it was very good. And there was evening, and there was morning—the sixth day. Thus the heavens and the earth were completed in all their vast array. By the seventh day God had finished the work he had been doing; so on the seventh day he rested from all his work. **Genesis 1 v 31 – 2 v 2**

God is a worker. He works and He rests from His work. And He still works. Jesus says: "My Father is always at his work to this very day, and I too am working" (John 5 v 17). God is a worker and Jesus is a worker (John 4 v 34 and 17 v 4).

And notice that God takes delight in His work. He looks at what He has done and says: "It is good". The writer of Proverbs describes the role of Wisdom in creation, and the New Testament sees this as a picture of Jesus. Proverbs says: "Then I was constantly at his side. I was filled with delight day after day, rejoicing always in his presence, rejoicing in his whole world and delighting in mankind" (Proverbs 8 v 30-31). Jesus was at the Father's side, crafting creation. And He takes delight in His work. Day after day He is filled with delight, rejoicing in God's workmanship.

Not only is God a worker, but He made humanity to share His work:

> So God created mankind in his own image, in the image of God he created them; male and female he created them. God blessed them and said to them, "Be fruitful and increase in number; fill the earth and subdue it. Rule over the fish in the sea and the birds in the sky and over every living creature that moves on the ground" ... The LORD God took the man and put him in the Garden of Eden to work it and take care of it. **Genesis 1 v 27-28; 2 v 15**

We are made in the image of God, and one of the things this means is ruling over creation as God's stewards.

On the first three days of creation God "separates". He separates light and dark, water and sky, sea and land. Genesis 1 v 2 says the world was *"formless and empty"*. In the first three days God orders or governs the chaos. Then on days four, five and six He fills the emptiness. He fills the sky with the sun, moon and stars. He fills the sky and seas with birds and fish. He fills the land with animals. Then God gives humanity the twin tasks of filling and governing the earth—the very things that He Himself was doing in creation. On each of the first three days of creation God "names" things. He names the "day" and "night", the "sky", the "land" and the "sea". But He does no naming on days four, five and six. Instead He gives humanity the task of naming the animals and birds (Genesis 2 v 19).

God created the world as a good, but unfinished project. Now He hands over His creation project to us. He calls on us to fill and subdue the world. This is often called **"the cultural mandate".** God gives us a mandate to create, invent, explore, discover, develop, produce, buy and sell. God has graciously invited us to participate with Him in the task of producing a beautiful world that brings Him glory.

Being made in God's image also means being relational, just as

God is relational. And through work we not only glorify God, we also provide for our families and contribute to our communities (Deuteronomy 14 v 28-29; Ephesians 4 v 28).

So work is commended in the Bible as a good thing. Work is not a necessary evil we have to endure. It is both a privilege and a blessing. This is why we find satisfaction and fulfilment in work. To work is to be part of what it means to be human. We find pleasure in a job well done. We delight in a product well made or a service well performed—something that works, something that is beautiful, something that will endure. It's a pleasure that we can all find in our work: the clean floor, the student who grasps an idea, the empty in-tray and the satisfied customer. That pleasure is an echo of the pleasure of God when He saw that all He had made was very good. When we find delight in a job well done, that delight is an echo of the delight that the Wisdom of God found in crafting the world.

Questions for reflection

- When a craftsman runs his hand over a finished piece of wood, he shares the joy of the Creator at the creation of the world. The satisfied customer. The productive workforce. The balanced books. The clean kitchen. The delivery made on time. The finished design.
  - *How do you share the joy of the Creator?*

- A common attitude in the modern world is that only the knowledge-based work of people like managers, teachers and designers is meaningful and fulfilling. We don't value the work of labourers and factory workers, or workers in the service sector like cleaners and waiters. Manual or mundane work is seen as undignified. Do you recognise this attitude in others? Has this attitude found a place in your own thinking?
  - *How does a biblical worldview challenge this thinking?*

- If you're a boss or in management, how can you make work satisfying and dignified for others? Health and safety legislation protects the bodies of workers, but we also need to care for the "humanness" of workers.
  - *How can you ensure work is not demeaning?*
  - *Are there ways in which you could make it interesting and fulfilling?*
  - *How can you honour those who work with you appropriately?*

Questions for reflection

2 NOTHING WORKS

Principle

Expect work to be boring, frustrating and hard.

Consider this

"How can we pray for one another?" asked John after the Bible study.

"You could pray I get a new job," said Mark.

"But you've not long been in this one."

"Yes, but it's just as bad as before. The customers treat me like dirt and my boss is a nightmare. And it's so boring. I want something more fulfilling."

"Wouldn't we all," thought John, thinking back on his day.

"That would be nice," he said to Mark. "But…"

"But what?"

Biblical background

Read Genesis 3 v 1-19

- How does sin affect the way human beings relate to one another?

- How does God's curse affect our work?

- How do you see these effects in your workplace?

Read all about it

In the world God created, work was meant to be fun, fulfilling and exciting. And often it still is. But we all know that work can also be frustrating, oppressive and hard. "How many people work here?" I once asked someone. "About half of them," was his quick-witted response. Or maybe you've said in exasperation: "Nothing works around here!" as the photocopier has jammed. Again.

Work can be frustrating

Imagine you're house-sitting for a friend. You're the person left in charge. But that doesn't mean you can do whatever you want. You have to look after your friend's property. That's exactly the situation in which God places us. He put us in charge of His world, but it remains *His* world and our job is to look after it. But instead we act as if it belongs to us. We're like squatters, taking possession of what is not ours.

Genesis 3 describes the rebellion of humanity against God and its consequences. And one of those consequences is that the ground is cursed. As a result, work now involves toil and sweat. Through *"painful toil"* we eat the fruit of the land. *"By the sweat of [our] brow"* we eat food. Work becomes a burden. It becomes frustrating, boring and stressful.

> When I surveyed all that my hands had done and what I had toiled to achieve, everything was meaningless, a chasing after the wind; nothing was gained under the sun ... So my heart began to despair over all my toilsome labour under the sun. For a person may labour with wisdom, knowledge and skill, and then they must leave all they own to another who has not toiled for it. This too is meaningless and a great misfortune. What do people get for all the toil and anxious striving with which they labour under the sun? All their days their work is grief and pain; even at night their minds do not rest. This too is meaningless. **Ecclesiastes 2 v 11, 20-23**

Endless emails, projects that go wrong, incompetent management, proposals that come to nothing—these are all part of working in a fallen world. Sometimes we find great delight in work—that's work as God intended. But often we find work frustrating—that's what work has become as a result of human rebellion against God.

Work can be oppressive

The frustrating nature of work in a fallen world is made worse by our sin and the sin of others. In our working life we come across difficult customers, conflict with colleagues or workplace bullies. The work environment is not always a happy one. Indeed, for many people work can feel demeaning. It makes the workplace a tough place to be a Christian. A friend of mine wrote to me:

> People get onto dirty jokes, sexist comments, assumptions of dishonesty or impropriety very early in a relationship at work. And if you do not play along, you will have to do so publicly. It can be near impossible. The skills needed are tough and the spiritual support, encouragement and exhortation to persevere are needed desperately.

Another expression of sin is the way some people avoid work:

> A sluggard says, "There's a lion in the road,
>   a fierce lion roaming the streets!"
> As a door turns on its hinges,
>   so a sluggard turns on his bed.
> A sluggard buries his hand in the dish;
>   he is too lazy to bring it back to his mouth.
>
> **Proverbs 26 v 13-15**

Paul says that such people should not eat. In others words, we should not confirm someone in their laziness by providing for their needs (see 2 Thessalonians 3 v 9-12; 1 Timothy 5 v 3-16).

But more often, poverty is the result of injustice and oppression. The writer of Proverbs describes the good world that God created as a world of predictable cause and effect in which hard work is rewarded:

> Those who work their land will have abundant food, but those who chase fantasies have no sense. **Proverbs 12 v 11**

But now God's good world is thoroughly corrupted by our rebellion. And that means that cause and effect do not always operate as God intended. Instead, the powerful use their position to exploit the poor. The labour of the poor and weak is often exploited.

> An unploughed field produces food for the poor, but injustice sweeps it away. **Proverbs 13 v 23**

And so work can be oppressive.

Work can be idolatrous

The prophet Isaiah condemns the trade of Tyre because it exploits other people, but also because the people of Tyre have used their trade to bring glory to *themselves* instead of bringing glory to God

(Isaiah 23 v 1-14). As we'll see, work can be a way in which we pursue our own glory in an idolatrous way, and look for fulfilment apart from God. Many people reach the top of their profession only to discover it doesn't bring the fulfilment they expected; because although we are made to work, we are also made for *more than* work. We are made for God Himself, and work can never be a satisfying substitute for God.

People today often seem to think they have a right to a job that is pleasant and fulfilling all the time. They become indignant when life isn't like that. They're like Christians who expect God to make them healthy all the time. We live in a fallen world that is not yet redeemed. So we should not be surprised if work is often boring or frustrating. We will face the temptation to be idle, to oppress others or to treat work as an idol. And even if we are able to resist those pressures, we will undoubtedly experience all those things among our work colleagues. The answer is to have a gospel-centred understanding of work, as a good thing ruined by the fall. And to set your sights on the new creation, when work will be a genuine delight.

Questions for reflection

- In what ways can your work be frustrating? In what ways can your work be oppressive? In what ways can your work be idolatrous?

- ***Read James 5 v 1-11.***
  - What does James say to people who *make* work oppressive?
  - What does James say to people who *find* work oppressive?

3 JESUS WORKS

Principle

Jesus transforms work, and work transforms the world.

Consider this

Pete loved his work. He was a carpet fitter, getting regular work from a couple of large retailers in town. He loved meeting customers. He loved working for himself. And he loved finishing the day at four. It gave him time for his family and for the church youth group he led.

But people kept telling him he could do better. A couple of people had suggested he expand, perhaps taking on a couple of staff so he could pitch for commercial contracts. Others suggested that someone with his abilities could do better for himself. Pete wasn't quite sure what they had in mind, but he suspected they meant a white-collar job where he would sit at a desk all day. Sometimes he felt as if he was doing something wrong. But he loved his work and the opportunities it brought.

How would he decide whether to go for expansion or not?

Janet loved her work. She had started out on a management programme for recent graduates in the local hospital and had been promoted a couple of times. She loved organising the chaos of hospital life and helping staff perform to the best of their ability. It brought some ethical dilemmas from time to time which could be challenging for her as a Christian, but she felt she had an opportunity to put across a biblical perspective.

And yet she felt a tension with church commitments. She was often late for her home-group meeting and she'd had to decline requests to volunteer with church programmes. One or two people had hinted to her that her work/life balance was wrong. Now a new opportunity had come up at work which really excited her. But she wondered how the others in her small group would respond.

How would she decide whether to go for promotion or not?

Biblical background

Read Hebrews 2 v 5-9

- Who is the writer talking about in verses 5-8?
- What is the glory of humanity?
- What is the failure of humanity?
- What difference does Jesus make?

Read all about it

God gave humanity the task of filling and subduing the earth. This is what gives meaning to our work. This is the glory of humanity—our crowning glory, according to the psalmist:

> You have made them a little lower than the angels
> and crowned them with glory and honour.
> You made them rulers over the works of your hands;
> you put everything under their feet. **Psalm 8 v 5-6**

But when the writer of Hebrews quotes Psalm 8, he also recognises that **this isn't the full picture.** Our rebellion against God means that

> At present we do not see everything subject to them.
>
> **Hebrews 2 v 8**

Adam was given the task of ruling over creation and tending the garden (Genesis 1 v 28; 2 v 15). But instead of ruling over the serpent, Adam allowed himself to be ruled by an animal. Our sin turns the world upside down. God's curse means work becomes a battle to control a hostile world. Not everything is subject to us. Not everything is rosy in the garden.

"We do not see everything subject to them. But we do see Jesus…" (Hebrews 2 v 8-9). We do not see Adam and his race fulfilling the task God gave them. But we do see Jesus, the new Adam. Adam was the beginning of humanity, and his sin affects us all because we are all born in Adam. For us, work is a frustrating battle. Jesus is the beginning of God's new humanity and His righteousness affects all who by faith are in Him.

Like Adam, Jesus was tempted by Satan, but He was faithful to God.

> At once the Spirit sent him out into the wilderness, and he was in the wilderness for forty days, being tempted by Satan. He was with the wild animals, and angels attended him. **Mark 1 v 12-13**

The presence of the wild animals is Mark's hint that creation is finally being tamed—that it is becoming subject again to humanity in the person of Jesus.

> For the creation waits in eager expectation for the children of God to be revealed. For the creation was subjected to frustration, not by its own choice, but by the will of the one who subjected it, in hope that the creation itself will be liberated from its bondage to decay and brought into the freedom and glory of the children of God.
>
> **Romans 8 v 19-21**

The redemption of humanity that has begun in Jesus will lead to the lifting of the curse over creation. We will be restored to our role as God's co-workers, ruling over and caring for creation. And through our redeemed labour, creation itself will also be redeemed.

Isaiah looks forward to a day when people will enjoy the fruit of their labour as God intended.

> They will build houses and dwell in them;
>   they will plant vineyards and eat their fruit.
> No longer will they build houses and others live in them,
>   or plant and others eat.
> For as the days of a tree,
>   so will be the days of my people;
> my chosen ones will long enjoy
>   the works of their hands. **Isaiah 65 v 21-22**

Although Isaiah announces the fall of the trading empire of Tyre, he also speaks of her restoration. Once again she will "ply her trade with all the kingdoms on the face of the earth". This time "her profit and her earnings will be set apart for the LORD" (23 v 17-18).

Trade with Tyre provided materials for Solomon's temple (1 Kings 5) and "satisfied many nations" (Ezekiel 27 v 33). Now Isaiah looks forward to the rebuilding of the temple when Tyre again will provide its building materials (Ezra 3 v 7). But he looks beyond this, too, to the day when the trading wealth of the nations will be used not for selfish, proud human ends, but for the glory of God and the provision of His people (Isaiah 60 v 5; Revelation 21 v 24-26). John says that God's redeemed people will serve Him, but without the threat of poverty or the heat of toil (Revelation 7 v 13-17).

Of course, the day when God's renewed humanity will renew the earth has not yet arrived. Only when Christ returns will the world be transformed. But in the meantime, Christians have a new vision for work and a new motivation for work. We may not be able to renew the whole world. But we *can* make a difference through our work.

Entrepreneurs and managers in particular have an opportunity to shape business towards blessing others. In this way they can generate what we might call "cultural profit"—benefits for the wider community. Not only the products they produce, but their employment and management practices, the design of their premises and the conduct of their meetings can all influence the wider culture, as well as pointing to the gospel message. Being in business gives an opportunity to exercise authority in a way that reflects the liberating and life-enhancing rule of God. You can treat employees, customers and suppliers as partners and your business blesses the wider community.

Some Christians have chosen not to pursue promotion or dropped to working only three or four days a week so they have time for mission through their local church. That's a great choice to make. Other Christians have pursued a career as an expression of ministry through the workplace. That's a great choice to make as well. What matters is making those choices for God's glory, not just for personal gain.

Joseph and Daniel both reached the top of their professions through faithful service. It meant that when the time came, they were in a position to serve God, bless His people and contribute to the advance of His saving purposes (Genesis 37 – 50; Daniel 1 – 6).

Esther, too, knew God had placed her in a position of influence. This young Jewish woman was married to the Persian king at just the moment when Haman, the leading court official, conceived a plan to destroy the Jews. Esther's uncle, Mordecai, says to her:

> "And who knows but that you have come to your royal position for such a time as this?" **Esther 4 v 14**

At huge risk to herself, Esther successfully approaches the king and saves her people.

And who knows but that you have come to your position in work for such a time as this?

Questions for reflection

In what position has God placed you?
What influence does it bring? How can you use that influence to serve God and bless others? What risks might this bring?

The gospel shapes the goal of business.
Growing a business is not an end in itself, whether for power, prestige or prosperity. Here are three models for a missional business:

1. **Lifestyle business:** Developing a business to support a missional lifestyle. This might involve earning sufficient income in four days a week to release time for mission or working in a role that creates evangelistic opportunities.
2. **Income generation:** Developing a business to generate income to support church planting.
3. **Economic and social renewal:** Developing a business to bless the city by creating employment, providing services, generating tax revenue and facilitating the establishment of new companies.

All three of these models can be combined to some extent. But some people will opt for one instead of another. They may, for example, not invest as much time as they could to maximise income (#2), so they have time for church planting (#1).

If you work for yourself or run a company, which of these models best describes your approach? How can you ensure these are genuine aims, and not a veneer for a selfish pursuit of power, prestige or prosperity?

The gospel shapes the goal of a career.
The same issues face Christian employees as they think about their careers. And models for a missional career reflect those for missional business. You could view your work as:

1. **Lifestyle career:** Opting for fewer responsibilities so you have time for church and mission, instead of progressing as far as you might.

2. **Income generation:** Developing a career to generate income to support church planting.

3. **Economic and social renewal:** Seeing your career as an opportunity to bless your wider community, apply Christian values and use your position to witness to Christ.

If you're an employee, which of these models best describes your approach? How can you ensure these are genuine aims, and not a veneer for a selfish pursuit of power, prestige or prosperity?

GOOD WORKS

Principle

Work as if Jesus is your boss.

Consider this

The alarm went off. Dwayne tried to ignore it. But it was no good. It was time to get up. He lay in bed feeling despondent. Tuesday morning. Still four days before the weekend. His wife was already up. He could hear her singing in the kitchen as she made a cup of tea. She was a real morning person.

Dwayne rolled over and closed his eyes. His job was boring and his boss was a pain, always going on about targets—as if anyone really cared how many service agreements anyone bought.

It was OK for his wife, she loved her work. But what reason did he have for getting out of bed?

Biblical background

Read Colossians 3 v 22 – 4 v 1

- What actions and attitudes does Paul expect from workers?
- What motivation does he give?
- What actions and attitudes does Paul expect from managers?
- Workers are to work as if Jesus is their boss. What about managers?

Read all about it

What's your boss like? Does he or she feel a bit like a tyrant? Or perhaps they leave you to get on with things on your own much of the time. Or maybe they're really supportive.

You may be your own boss. But it's still worth asking the question: "What's your boss like?" If you're driven by the need to succeed, then you may be a tyrannical boss *over yourself* (and perhaps also over your employees).

The attitude of our boss can have a big impact on the way we feel about our work.

When Paul writes to the Thessalonians, he tells them to avoid Christians who are idle. He reminds them of his own example when he was among them.

> For you yourselves know how you ought to follow our example. We were not idle when we were with you, nor did we eat anyone's food without paying for it. On the contrary, we worked night and day, labouring and toiling so that we would not be a burden to any of you. We did this, not because we do not have the right to such help, but in order to offer ourselves as a model for you to imitate.
>
> **2 Thessalonians 3 v 7-9**

Paul could have received money from them for his ministry. But he chose to work *night and day* because he wanted to set them an example of hard work and not being a burden to others (see also Acts 20 v 33-35).

Work and the grace of God

Christians should find a renewed commitment to hard work. It's not that we work hard to win God's approval. We receive God's approval as a gift.

In the world around us, this is how the equation tends to work:

activity (what we do) ⇨ identity (who we are)

In other words, **who I am is based on what I do**. I'm a successful business person if I succeed in business. I'm a good mother if I have lovely children. I'm a professional if I gain the necessary qualifications. I'm a good worker if I work hard.

But the grace of God turns this whole way of thinking upside down in the most counter-intuitive of ways.

> For it is by grace you have been saved, through faith—and this is not from yourselves, it is the gift of God—not by works, so that no one can boast. For we are God's handiwork, created in Christ Jesus to do good works, which God prepared in advance for us to do.
>
> **Ephesians 2 v 8-10**

If activity leads to identity, then I can be saved only if and when I do good works. But it's not my works that make me who I am, but God's work. We are *God's handiwork*. It's Christ's work on the cross that saves me, that makes me a saved person approved by God.

The grace of God turns the world's way upside down. Instead of activity (what we do) ⇨ identity (who we are), with the grace of God:

identity (who I am) ⇨ activity (what I do)

God makes me a good person (a person declared righteous in His sight) through Christ. In Christ I am someone who does good works. My good works don't make me who I am. Instead they're the natural expression of who I am as a result of God's work.

You can't make a tree into an apple tree by gluing apples onto it. But if a tree is an apple tree then *it will produce apples*—of course it will; that's what apple trees do. In the same way, you can't make yourself a good person, by gluing good works on to your life. But if you're a good person then you'll produce good works—of course you will; that's what good people do.

What's the result of Christ's work for us and the Spirit's work in us? We are "created in Christ Jesus to do good works, which God prepared in advance for us to do." In the workplace (as in the rest of life) we will do good work.

Work and the glory of God

But what is the source of this renewed commitment to work? It is that Christians have rediscovered that work can be done for the glory of God.

> Slaves, obey your earthly masters in everything; and do it, not only when their eye is on you and to curry their favour, but with sincerity of heart and reverence for the Lord. Whatever you do, work at it with all your heart, as working for the Lord, not for human masters, since you know that you will receive an inheritance from the Lord as a reward. It is the Lord Christ you are serving. **Colossians 3 v 22-24**

We work "with sincerity of heart and reverence for the Lord". We work "as working for the Lord". We look to "a reward" from him. "It is the Lord Christ we are serving." Workers are to work as if Jesus is their boss. But so are bosses: "Masters, provide your slaves with what is right and fair, because you know that you also have a Master in heaven" (Colossians 4 v 1). Paul does not simply say we can take delight in our work. We can also take delight in the fact that God takes delight in our work.

"Why aren't you working?" said a boss to one of his employees. "Because I didn't see you coming." It's very easy to work hard or follow the right procedures when our boss can see us, but cut corners when they're not around. But we're to work as if Jesus is our boss and Jesus sees us all the time. Even when no-one else recognises what we do, we can find pleasure in knowing that we are pleasing God.

Questions for reflection

- How does working as if Christ is your boss change your approach to work?

- List the qualities that make someone a good worker. List the qualities that make someone a good manager. How many of these are Christian virtues?

- Do Christians make better employees? Should they? Does it depend on the mix of ability and attitude required for a job?

- Do Christians make better managers? Should they?

PART TWO

TRANSFORMING WORK

5 I'M WORRIED ABOUT MY WORK

Principle

As I trust God's control, I won't fear problems.

Consider this

Carlos surveyed the damage. The car was a write-off, but at least he was OK and his equipment seemed intact. But what was he going to do now?

He was supposed to be at a wedding in an hour's time and people don't take kindly to being let down by their photographer. Could he just leave the car by the roadside? And how was he going to get to the church?

What was he going to do?

"Think solutions." That's what Amanda's boss always said. "Think solutions." The worst of it was she knew it was her fault. Of course she should have checked whether any of the guests were vegetarians, but someone how she'd missed it.

Now four people wanted the vegetarian option and she didn't have one. Omelette? Not for an up-market wedding and not at the price the clients were paying. Her heart was racing. Then one of the waitresses told her they were running out of canapés.

What was she going to do?

Biblical background
Read Mark 4 v 35-41

- What's the problem the disciples face?
- What does Jesus say is their problem?
- When do you feel anxious about work?
- What's the answer to fear?

Read all about it

Do you ever worry about your work? Of course you do. I suspect most of us do from time to time.

According to Murphy's Law: *what can go wrong, will go wrong*. That may be a little on the pessimistic side. But certainly plenty of things in the workplace do go wrong. Things can't be mended and parts go missing. Pipes spring leaks and circuits blow fuses. Sales fall through and deadlines get missed. Customers get irate and bosses become unreasonable. And that's just on Monday!

The workplace can be a place of extreme stress. It might be the work itself. You can't do what you're supposed to do—at least, not in the timescale required. Maybe you've made a mistake or the task is beyond your abilities. Maybe it's colleagues or suppliers who've let you down. Or it might be other people who make work stressful: awkward colleagues, difficult customers, an overbearing boss.

What do we do in those moments of stress?

There are lots of tools to help us cope with the pressures of work—emails, online calendars, task lists, wall charts, smart phones. And there is huge value in many of these. But we need to beware the illusion that we can always be in control.

Think about what happens if we think we're in control or that we can tackle every problem simply with more effort.

- We'll tend to overwork to ensure everything is under our control.
- We'll put excessive pressure on co-workers to ensure everything is under control.
- We'll grow anxious when things don't feel under our control.

In 4 v 35-41 Mark describes an evening when Jesus was in a boat with His disciples. A number of the disciples were fishermen by trade. So this was their working environment. Jesus had spent the day preaching. Perhaps the disciples felt relieved to be doing a task they knew how to do. This was their area of competency.

But then a furious storm comes up. Soon their workplace is in chaos! They are figuratively out of their depth and it is starting to look as if they might be literally out of their depth!

In this chaos Jesus simply rebukes the storm: "Quiet! Be Still!" And immediately everything is calm. Jesus is in control. Complete control.

> He said to his disciples, "Why are you so afraid? Do you still have no faith?"

It seems a bit harsh. After all, some of the disciples were experienced fishermen. Surely their assessment of the storm was accurate. And indeed it was. It was their assessment of Jesus that was inaccurate. "Who is this?" they ask themselves. If they had known the answer to that question, then faith would have replaced fear.

What problems do you face at work? What "storms'? Your assessment of your work problems may be accurate. It may be chaos.

Disaster may be approaching. But what about your assessment of Jesus? What's your answer to the question, *"Who is this?"*

Here's the truth that we need to hang on to: **Jesus is in control of our work situations. He does answer prayer and He can sort out work problems.**

That doesn't mean every "storm" will be calmed or every disaster averted. Projects will still fail, jobs will go wrong, colleagues will let us down. We may even get fired. **But Jesus is in control.** And His purposes for us are *always* good. It's not always the "good" we might choose for ourselves. Sometimes it's even better. For God's purpose for us is that we might know Him and enjoy Him and become like Him (Romans 8 v 28-30).

Hebrews 12 v 4-11 says that God disciplines his children. It's not that He punishes us for our failure—He is always gracious towards us, and all the punishment has been taken by Jesus on the cross. Instead, think of it like an induction programme. A new employee is often given a programme of activities to introduce them to a new company, perhaps doing a number of different roles in the firm so they understand the business. God has designed a programme of activities to prepare you for heaven. That programme of activities is called life. All its ups and downs are specially selected by God to lovingly shape you into a good servant and a happy child of God. The current problems you face at work are part of that programme.

> No discipline seems pleasant at the time, but painful. Later on, however, it produces a harvest of righteousness and peace for those who have been trained by it. **Hebrews 12 v 11**

Questions for reflection

- How would remembering God's sovereign care help Carlos and Amanda? What difference might their colleagues or clients notice?

- Do you pray for your work? If not, why not?

- Do you pray during work as problems or opportunities arise? Are there other Christians in your workplace with whom you could pray?

6 I'M AFRAID OF MY BOSS

Principle

As I seek God's approval, I won't fear people.

Consider this

Clara, a member of Karen's house group, was unwell. Karen was going to go round in the evening to cook her a meal. She was thinking about what she was going make and the ingredients she would buy on the way home from work.

If she left at five, she could be at the supermarket by quarter past, at Clara's shortly after six, and the meal could be ready by seven.

Then her boss stopped at her desk. "Can you prepare the revised sales figure for me?"

"That sounds like a question," thought Karen. But she knew it was really an order.

"Can I do them tomorrow morning?" Karen asked.

"Sorry. I need them for a meeting at nine."

"What can I do?" thought Karen. "I'll just have to let Clara down."

Biblical background
Read Daniel 3

- What kind of boss is Nebuchadnezzar?
- What enables Shadrach, Meshach and Abednego to do the right thing?
- What is the outcome of the story?
- What alternative outcome do Shadrach, Meshach and Abednego contemplate in verse 18?
- What lessons are there for you in this?

Read all about it

This is one major workplace dilemma. Shadrach, Meshach and Abednego are employed in the Babylonian civil service. Nebuchadnezzar organises a massive work conference for all his employees. On the agenda is just one thing: they must all express their allegiance to the company by bowing down before his 30-foot high image. And one more thing: those who refuse will be burnt in a furnace.

Shadrach, Meshach and Abednego are faithful to the God of Israel, so they refuse to bow before Nebuchadnezzar's image. "We do not need to defend ourselves before you in this matter" (3 v 16). It's not that they're indifferent to Nebuchadnezzar's opinion. They're respectful to him throughout the story and keep calling him "Your Majesty" (see 3 v 17, 18, 24). They're not surly workers who slack off at every opportunity or gossip about their boss behind his back. They've already proven themselves to be conscientious workers (1 v 7, 18-20).

Nebuchadnezzar's opinion matters to them—but not as much

as God's opinion. They talk about "the God we serve". They serve Nebuchadnezzar—but their allegiance to God comes first. So "in this matter", Nebuchadnezzar's opinion will always come second.

The fear of other people is a big issue in the workplace. Often it will be fear of our boss. But there might be other co-workers whose approval we crave or whose rejection we fear.

There's nothing wrong with wanting to be liked or to win other people's approval. It's a strange person who's indifferent to these things. But the desire for approval and the fear of rejection can very easily control us. And then it's a problem. Here are some possible symptoms:

- Not being able to say "No" to work demands.
- Exaggerating your achievements or understating your failings.
- Creating a difference between your private life and your public life, or between your church persona and your work persona.
- Keeping quiet about being a Christian for fear of being ridiculed or uncool.
- Lying to cover up your mistakes or shortcomings.
- Pretending to be someone you're not in order to fit in, or hiding the person you really are.
- Not taking opportunities to talk about Jesus, because you're worried about what people might think.

The Bible calls this "the fear of man". It's solution is simple: **the fear of God.** Or to put it another way, the more we grasp the majesty, glory, holiness, mercy, love, judgment and beauty of God, the more His opinion will matter to us more than anyone else's.

This was Shadrach, Meshach and Abednego's secret. Nebuchadnezzar was a scary man. He became "furious with rage" (3 v 13, 19). He orders the furnace to be made seven times hotter than normal—so hot it roasts the soldiers who carry out the king's orders to throw the three men in. But Shadrach, Meshach and Abednego recognise that God is even more terrifying. "What god will be able to rescue you from my hand?" asks Nebuchadnezzar. But Shadrach, Meshach and Abednego know that the true God can deliver them (3 v 17) and, even if He doesn't, they would still rather disobey Nebuchadnezzar than the living God (3 v 18).

Jesus says:

> "I tell you, my friends, do not be afraid of those who kill the body and after that can do no more. But I will show you whom you should fear: fear him who, after your body has been killed, has authority to throw you into hell. Yes, I tell you, fear him."
>
> **Luke 12 v 4-5**

The answer to the fear of man is the fear of God. Jesus' logic is stark. The worst any human being can do to you is kill your body. Beyond that, there's nothing more they can do. But God can send you to an eternal death in hell.

The answer is to put the fear of people in a right perspective. When we fear someone's rejection, that person looms large in our minds. Their opinion counts for everything. We lose perspective. But when we see the majesty, holiness, glory, love, mercy, power and kindness of God, then we start to regain a proper perspective.

People might still get upset or angry with us. Shadrach, Meshach and Abednego were willing to get fired—and fried (3 v 17-18)! But the anger of others won't affect us in the same ways when we realise God's approval is what really matters.

And here's the lovely thing: **we have God's approval already in Christ.** In Christ God declares us righteous and adopts us into His family. Nothing we can do—good or bad—can undo the fact that we are God's sons and daughters. And nothing people can do to us can change that reality either.

Here's how this works in practice for me. When I realise my behaviour or emotions are being unhelpfully affected by someone's opinion, I often turn to Psalm 27 v 1:

The LORD is my light and my salvation—
whom shall I fear?
The LORD is the stronghold of my life—
of whom shall I be afraid?

I repeated it over and over again to myself, all the time meditating on what it says. "Who lights up my life? Who offers me salvation? Who is my stronghold? Not this human being whose opinion seems to matter so much to me. No, it's the Lord. Whom shall I fear? The only person I should fear is God and He is my loving Father."

A right perspective on God frees us to serve other people better. Without it, we only serve them for what we get out of it—winning their approval or avoiding their rejection. But putting God first frees us to serve other people in love.

Questions for reflection

- One major Christian employer said Christians often make bad managers, because they think Christians should always be "nice"—never confronting people, always forgiving, always affirming. Is this your experience? What do you make of this attitude?

- How can the fear of God free us to be good managers?

? People who are not trusting in God's greatness often over-intervene, because they feel the need to control everything. People who are not looking to God for approval often under-intervene, because they want everyone to like them. Do you tend to over-intervene or under-intervene?

? How can faith in God help you get this balance right?

7 I CAN'T BEAR TO FAIL

Principle

As I receive God's grace, I won't fear failure.

Consider this

Ahmed sat behind the wheel, waiting at the lights. He felt weary. His team had failed to hit their sales targets again. The area sales manager had been with him all afternoon. He'd gone on and on about their neighbouring branch, about how well it was doing, what a dynamic team they were. Ahmed had been on his colleagues' backs all month. But the only difference it had made was to increase their resentment towards him. He felt rubbish as he inched his way through the rush-hour traffic.

He was still feeling rubbish as he sat drinking a mug of tea after the Bible study with his small group. He'd not said much all evening. He didn't feel like contributing—and didn't have much to offer tonight in any case. "You OK?" asked George.

Ahmed thought as he sipped his tea. Should he give George the whole story? But what would be the point? After all, what could George say or do that would help?

Biblical background

Read Titus 2 v 9-15

- How should Christian workers behave?
- What will create this behaviour in Christians?

Read Titus 3 v 1-8

- What is it that gives Christians their identity and worth?
- What kind of behaviour does this lead to?

Read all about it

In the medieval worldview, a person proved themselves right before God through religious works. And the top way to do that, people thought, was through spiritual disciplines and contemplation. So the very best thing to do was to become a monk or a nun. You left behind the real world of ordinary work and went off to pray.

The great driving force behind the Protestant Reformation was a rediscovery of what the Bible actually says about being right with God. The Bible says that we become right with God through what God has done—and not at all through what we do. "[God our Saviour] saved us," says Paul in Titus 3 v 5-7, "not because of righteous things we had done, but because of his mercy ... so that, having been justified by his grace, we might become heirs having the hope of eternal life."

This meant you didn't need to go off into a monastery to become right with God. You could serve God right where you were. God made you right with Him as a gracious gift, and you could then live out your new identity in everyday life.

People often talk about the "Protestant work ethic". The Protestant work ethic is the commitment to ordinary work that arose because of the value given to all of life by the Reformation. Being a Christian was not about escaping the world of manual work, but serving God in the real world.

Today, people often claim that the Protestant work ethic is the reason for our stress-filled world of modern work. But the problem is not the Protestant work ethic as rediscovered by the reformers. The problem is what happened next in the story.

Justification by work

In the Bible's vision of life, work is just *one way* in which you can serve God. Rest is another way. We both work and rest to the glory of God. What mattered was God and His glory. What mattered was what God has done for us, making us right with Him through the death of Jesus.

But when secularisation came along, God was taken out of the picture.

Now, we find meaning through work itself. Our sense of being a person of worth is found not through our relationship with God, but through work. In other words, we seek, unconsciously, to justify ourselves through our secular jobs or roles. Just think about how people would answer these questions: "What do you do?" and "What are you worth?" Most would answer these with a job title and a salary figure. Work has become, for many people, the measure of who they are. It's our identification of our role and value with work that creates the drive to succeed. Our identity depends on it.

The information revolution has in some respects made this even worse. Work, for many people, has become much more interesting. We're not just on a factory production line doing the same thing over and over again. And that's good news. Many more people now enjoy more interesting jobs.

But it's also created even greater expectations. We want work itself to be fulfilling. The value of work is measured by the sense of self-fulfilment it brings. A generation ago people took pride in working, even at monotonous jobs, because they were providing for their families and serving the wider community. Work was judged by the service it rendered to others.

But now it's all about me. Work is judged by the service it renders to me, the worker. We look for "salvation" (meaning, fulfilment and honour) through "rewarding" jobs. Management gurus no longer simply tell us how to chair a good meeting or make a good product. Now they promise to release your inner potential, so you can find meaning and fulfilment. They offer salvation from within. Companies now speak using the religious language of identity, meaning, mission and values. This is not an accident.

If we see work as salvation, as the means by which we will find identity or fulfilment, then failure at work will be a devastating experience. Of course it will, because my identity depends on my being a "success". On a good day, you'll be filled with pride at all you've achieved. You'll think of yourself as a "self-made man or woman". And a bad day at work will leave you in ruins, because your very self is at stake.

Justification by grace

> We who are Jews by birth and not sinful Gentiles know that a person is not justified by the works of the law, but by faith in Jesus Christ. So we, too, have put our faith in Christ Jesus that we may be justified by faith in Christ and not by the works of the law, because by the works of the law no one will be justified. **Galatians 2 v 15-16**

By *"works of the law"*, Paul means Jewish religious duties. But the same principle applies to our modern view of work. A person is not justified by work, we might say. Instead we are justified by faith in Christ. That's a shorthand way of saying that we are justified by trusting in the work Christ has done on the cross, by being united with Him through faith so that His death is our death, His life is our life and His approval before God is our approval before God.

Finding our identity in Christ helps free us from our insecurities. We are children of God, and that can't be altered by a good day at work or a day filled with mistakes and failures. When we look to our jobs to find our identity, it tends to have an unhealthy effect on work relationships. But, when we are secure in our identity in Christ, we are able to work in an atmosphere of openness and honesty, which healthy teams need to thrive. It enables us to ask questions like: "Are we doing well?" and "How could we improve?", without being crushed by the discovery that we are failing in some way.

When your work is interesting and fulfilling, count it a great blessing. But don't make it the basis of your identity. If your work is mundane or frustrating, then enjoy the fact that you're a child of God through faith in Christ and do your work to His glory.

Questions for reflection

A common cause of tension in the workplace is insecurity, especially when it's a manager who is insecure. People worry about their standing, their future, their reputation. It can make them:

- **Overbearing** as they push people to perform.
- **Defensive** as they reject any criticism.
- **Ineffectual** as they refuse to confront co-workers.

Which of these things do you recognise in your colleagues? What about yourself? How does the gospel free us from these insecurities, so we can be good workers?

8 I FIND IT HARD TO STOP

Principle

As I trust God's provision, I can balance work and rest over a week.

Consider this

Paul leaned back in his chair and yawned. It was already past six, and he reckoned it would be another half hour at least before the in-tray was empty. Home by 7.30 perhaps? He felt guilty for not putting the children to bed again. But what could he do?

Gloria sat down in the armchair with a mug of tea. It was 7.30pm. She took a couple of sips of tea and then glanced across at her smartphone. She hated having emails in her inbox. When her inbox was empty she felt as if she was on top of things. She reached over to pick it up. "Oh no you don't!", shouted her husband. "No emails."

"You don't understand," she replied. She hated the thought of an unanswered email. She could feel the tension mounting between them as she thumbed the button—but what could she do?

Biblical background
Read Luke 12 v 22-34

- What point is Jesus making when He reminds us that flowers don't do any work?

- What things are pagans busy running after?

- What will prevent us running around and being over busy?

Read all about it

A few years ago, researchers at Oxford University Press analysed the language used in newspapers, journals and blogs. Here are the top ten nouns we use in reverse order: "hand', "life', "world', "man', "thing", "day", "way", "year", "person" and, top of the list, "time". Not only is "time" at number one, but "year" is third, "day" is fifth and "week" is 17th. The word "work" is the 15th most frequently used noun, but "play" and "rest" didn't even feature in the top 100.

Have you felt *too* busy in the last year, the last month, the last week? It's a big issue in our culture. We seem to have a workaholic culture and work-life balance is becoming a big concern. It's also a big issue affecting the church. We want to spend more time praying, reading our Bibles, serving the church and evangelising our community—but we don't have time.

What's a balance between work and rest?

Some people rest to work—the only value they see in rest is making work more productive. Some people work to rest—the only value in work is earning an income to enjoy leisure. But according to the Bible, work is good and rest is good. Scripture commends hard work (Proverbs 6 v 6-11; 2 Thessalonians 3 v 6-13). But it also commends rest (Exodus 20 v 8-11).

The fourth commandment in Exodus 20 v 8-11 says we are to rest because God Himself rested. Rest is godly, because it's God-like. The fourth commandment in Deuteronomy 5 v 12-15 says the Israelites are to rest, because God redeemed them from slavery in Egypt. The Sabbath day is an expression of being saved *from* the slavery of work without rest under Pharaoh *for* joyful service and blessing under God's reign. It is also an expression of trust in God's provision, because it urges us to take a day off when we're not productive.

The Sabbath day was a sign of the covenant with Moses (Exodus 31 v 12-17) and a pointer to the coming rest that Jesus offers us. Christians are no longer under the letter of the Mosaic law (see Romans 7 v 6; 1 Corinthians 9 v 20-21; Hebrews 8 v 13). But the Sabbath principle of balancing work and rest over a seven-day period still has a lot to teach our workaholic culture. We often overwork throughout the year and then try to load all our rest into a two-week holiday. But the healthy pattern is a balance of work and rest over a week.

How can we achieve a balance between work and rest?

For most of us, busyness is self-induced. It's not that we decide in the morning: "Today I'm going to overwork". But our busyness is the result of choices we make and the desires we nurture.

We don't often think of it like that. We blame our bosses or the economy or the government or our spouses. "You don't understand," you may be thinking. "I have responsibilities. I have to stay late. I have to do overtime. There's so much to do. There just aren't enough hours in the day." But God put 24 hours in each day and God doesn't make mistakes. So the problem is not that there aren't enough hours in the day. The problem is that you're trying to do too much—more than God expects.

Provision for your identity

Some of us are busy, as we saw in the last chapter, because we find identity in our work. On the first ever management training course I attended we were given some advice which I've always remembered: "Don't tell people how busy you are, because what they'll hear is, 'I don't have time for you'." So why do we keep telling people how busy we are? What are we trying to communicate? "I'm doing a good job; I'm worth my pay; I'm important; I matter; you should admire me; you should value me."

If you're busy trying to prove yourself, then you'll always be busy. You'll never get the job done—because you can't prove yourself. You'll be like a dog chasing its tail. Jesus cried on the cross: "It is finished". The job is done. There is full atonement. There is nothing left for you to do. Here's what you need to do about the busyness that comes from trying to prove yourself: **nothing**—everything has already been done.

Again, as we've seen, some of us are busy because we can't say "No". We crave people's approval or we fear people's rejection. The good news is that God is bigger, and living for Him sets us free from being controlled by other people's approval or disapproval.

Provision for your needs

Some of us are busy because we need to be in control. We worry about the future. "We don't need the money now, but who knows what the future may bring?" we may say. Or we worry about people. We think they need us. But we're not in control of the world and we can't solve every problem. We're not saviours and we're not God. But the good news is that God is God! We have a Father in heaven, who controls the world and cares for His people.

Some of us are busy because we think we need the money. But need it for what? Most of don't need extra money to make ends meet. We certainly don't need it to be happy (since it's actually making us stressed). We "need" it because we think an extra holiday, a flashier car, a bigger house will make us happy. But true joy comes from knowing God. "Life," said Jesus, "does not consist in the abundance of possessions" (Luke 12 v 15). Think about the contented people you know and see whether Jesus isn't right.

When Jesus tells us not to run after the things that make the pagan world so busy, He chides us for our little faith (Luke 12 v 28). He invites us to:

> "consider how the wild flowers grow. They do not labour or spin. Yet I tell you, not even Solomon in all his splendour was dressed like one of these." (Luke 12 v 27)

Labour is good, but labour which betrays a lack of trust in God's ability to provide for His children is idolatrous. And you can spot idolatrous busyness, because it will eventually cause harm—in our bodies, in our families, in our churches and in our relationship with God. Only through faith in the God who dresses flowers can we seek first the kingdom of God (v 31). We can't add a single hour to our lives, let alone one to every day (v 25). But there is no need to worry. Our heavenly Father is in control. He requires of us no more than we can do in the time He gives us. And the problems we think we need more time to fix are all within His sovereign care.

Questions for reflection

Think about your busyness.

How can I use my time more efficiently?
In what ways do you waste time? How do you procrastinate? Do you get involved in things you don't need to? What time of day is best for you to do work requiring lots of concentration?

Questions for reflection

What are my priorities?

What are you busy doing? What are your priorities and are they what you spend most of your time doing? Does the urgent crowd out the important? What can you leave undone? Above all, what does it mean for you to put first the kingdom of God?

What creates the pressure for you to do more than God expects?

The person responsible for your busyness is you. So the core of the problem lies in your heart. Are you too busy because:

- you're trying to prove yourself?
- you're driven by other people's expectations?
- you're trying to have everything under control?
- you're trying to secure your future?
- Yyou're trying to live a materialistic version of the good life?

What is it in each of these desires that's potentially idolatrous? How does Jesus offer a better way?

9 I CAN'T GET ALONG WITH THEM

Principle

Conflict is an opportunity to repent of selfish desires or demonstrate grace.

Consider this

"How was work today?" asked John.

Barry and Sue smiled at each other. "He swore at his boss today," said Sue. Barry looked sheepish. "I couldn't help it. He's such a…" He paused, choosing his words carefully. "…pain in the neck."

"What do you mean?"

"He's always undermining me. I know he gets it from the management, but nothing's ever good enough. Like today, I did one thing wrong and he's shrieking at me—in front of everyone. So, well, I gave as good as I got. I know I shouldn't have sworn. But I couldn't help it. He's such a… Well, you know."

"I do know," laughed John. "But…"

Biblical background

Read James 3 v 13-18.

- What's the result of envy and selfish ambition?

- What's the result of humility?

Read James 4 v 1-12.

- What's the cause of conflict?

- What's the solution to conflict?

Read all about it

"I'm not sure how long I can stay in my job. It's all so toxic. I can't stand the back-biting, the gossip, the put-downs, the competition."

I've heard enough comments like these to realise that you're the exception if relationships are good in your workplace. Work throws a group of sinners together in close proximity and then often puts them under intense pressure. Most of the time, finding a different job won't solve the problem. You'll just find another group of people who are difficult to get along with.

Battles within

Conflict, of course, is always someone else's fault. At least, that's how we see it. If I get angry or lose my temper, then it's because of the actions of someone else. I was provoked. My response was inevitable. My behaviour was reasonable. It was their behaviour that was unreasonable.

But the Bible says the cause of conflict is within:

> What causes fights and quarrels among you? Don't they come from your desires that battle within you? **James 4 v 1**

The root of conflict in the workplace is the idolatrous desires of our hearts. When those desires are thwarted or threatened, we react. We may react with fighting or quarrels. We may react with anger, sulking, bitterness, resentment, complaining.

The Bible says that the source of all human behaviour and emotions is the heart. All our actions flow from the heart (Mark 7 v 20-23; Luke 6 v 43-45; Romans 1 v 21-25; Ephesians 4 v 17-24). The pressures of the workplace, or the behaviour of your colleagues, may create the circumstances that trigger your idolatrous desires. But they're never the cause:

> When tempted, no-one should say, "God is tempting me." For God cannot be tempted by evil, nor does he tempt anyone; but each person is tempted when they are dragged away by their own evil desire and enticed. **James 1 v 13-14**

What our colleagues, clients or the company do is not under our control. **But how we respond is down to us.**

A sinful desire is not just a desire for a bad thing. It can also be a desire for a good thing which has become bigger than God. To want to be respected by your colleagues, succeed in business, leave on time, or find fulfilment in work are all good things to desire. But if my work makes me angry or bitter, then my desire for respect or success or leisure or fulfilment has grown too big—bigger than my desire for God. As a result, I can't be content with God's sovereignty over my life.

So when you have an argument at work, or a colleague's behaviour annoys you, or you feel resentful toward your employers, try to work out those underlying idolatrous desires.

I have a desire for order. That's a good desire. It generally makes organisations run well. But that desire can be idolatrous. If people don't do things my way, I can readily get annoyed. If my email inbox is full, then I get frustrated. That frustration is the sign that something is wrong—not with the system or with other people, but with me!

The bad fruit in my behaviour is a sign of a bad root in my heart (Luke 6 v 43-45). I want life to be ordered my way. I want it to be all about me. And so, when I don't get my way then I get annoyed. So I need to learn again that God is the one who matters. And God is the one who is sovereign.

Answering the following questions may help you understand more deeply what is going on in yourself.

1. When do you respond badly in the workplace?
What triggers your response? Can you spot any patterns? You might want to consider one particular incident or a pattern of behaviour. Identifying the points at which you get angry or bitter or resentful enables you to think about what you wanted in that situation.

2. How do you respond badly?
People express themselves in many different ways: some shout or stamp their feet; some go in for snide or sarcastic remarks; some bottle it up and then explode; some withdraw or sulk. Some people may not see their reactions as sinful, because they only associate anger with outbursts of rage. You may see yourself as a calm person, because you don't shout and scream. But your inner attitude exhibits itself in the comments you make or your indifference to others.

3. What happens when you act badly?

Wisdom is revealed in a good life and deeds done in humility (James 3 v 13). It's *"peace-loving, considerate, submissive, full of mercy and good fruit, impartial and sincere"* (3 v 17). Envy and self-ambition, in contrast, produce "disorder and every evil practice" (3 v 16). Retell the story or stories of your conflict. Explore the results of your behaviour or response. What harmful fruit are your actions producing in your workplace and work relationships?

4. Why do you act badly?

One of the ironies of conflict situations is that we blame the other party for *their* actions and we blame the other party for *our* actions as well! "They're angry because they're in the wrong and I'm angry because they're in the wrong." Our sinful instinct is to judge the other party and not ourselves. But James says, in effect: *"Don't play God. Don't make yourself the judge"* (James 4 v 11-12; Matthew 7 v 1-5.) Even if the other person was worse than us, our responsibility is to repent of playing God.

- Ask yourself: "What am I thinking?" and "What do I really want?" to identify your failure to trust God as you should and the idolatrous desires that control your heart. Ask yourself: "What makes me want to wage war" (4 v 1-2) when Christ's rule should make me want to make peace (3 v 17-18)? We act badly because we're not getting something that we want. This desire has won the battle for control of our hearts (4 v 1) leading to spiritual adultery (4 v 4).
- Pray for the wisdom to identify the desires behind your behaviour (1 v 5; 3 v 13-18).
- Humble yourself before God (4 v 6-7).
- Repent of your desires and behaviour (4 v 10).

Some conflict is our fault. More often we contribute to conflict as other people trigger our selfish reactions. But sometimes we're innocent. What do we do in those situations? Remember this: **All sin is punished by God.** You don't have to fight for justice, because

God will see justice is done. He might bring judgment at the final day. If the person involved is a Christian, then God has brought judgment at the cross. Either way, sin is punished.

But this reminds us, too, that *our* sin was punished at the cross. Jesus took the penalty for sin that we deserve. We may be innocent in this situation, but we're not innocent people. We're guilty sinners—just like the people we find hard to work with. But God has been amazingly gracious to us. It's hard to be angry with other people when you stand at the cross.

Questions for reflection

Reflect on a recent occasion when there was conflict in your workplace or a time when you were resentful. Or reflect on a pattern of problem behaviour. Use the framework above to identify the heart desires that caused your behaviour, and to identify the appropriate response.

? When did you respond badly to your colleague?

- How did you respond badly?
- What happened when you acted badly?
- Why did you act badly?

Teams work best when:

- they have a common purpose with clear goals
- value the diversity within the team
- co-operate rather than compete with one another

? What needs to happen in your heart for you to be a good team member? Identify how these principles are reflected in Paul's teaching on the body of Christ in 1 Corinthians 12.

PART THREE

MISSION WORK

10 BLESSING

Principle

Work out how your work serves other people.

Consider this

Barry was whistling (badly) in the kitchen as he made the tea.

"You're in a good mood," said John.

"Yes, I am," replied Barry. "Had a great day at work."

"Really? That's great. What's going on? Have you got a new boss?"

"No. Well sort of." Barry laughed. "What you said about Jesus being my boss really helped. I still get hassle from 'my other boss'. But I tell myself, 'You've done a good job today and Jesus is pleased with that.'"

"That's brilliant."

"And there's another thing. I've started thinking about all the people who'll be living in the houses we're building. I know it sounds weird, but I think of them turning on my radiators and being warm!"

"I love it," said John. "That's a great attitude."

"Yeah, but what about me?" chipped in Sandra. "No-one sees the accounts I do, except my boss—and he's a miserable so-and-so."

Biblical background
Read Mark 12 v 28-34.

- How can we love God through our work?

- How can we love our neighbour through our work?

Read all about it

Working to the glory of God is all well and good. But what does it actually mean? Does it just mean sharing the gospel with people at work? Is that how God is glorified in the workplace? Does it mean earning money that I can give to gospel work? Does it means praying about my work?

It can certainly include all these things. But there's more to it than that. They all make work the *context* for glorying God, but not the *content* of God-glorifying activity. Glorifying God while at work is one thing. Glorifying God *through* your work is another.

We've already seen that God made us to glorify Him through work as we fill and subdue the earth. God Himself is a worker who finds pleasure in what He's made and we glorify Him when we find pleasure in our work.

In Genesis 11, the people of the world gather together "to make a name" for themselves. Instead of scattering to fill the earth, they come together. And instead of working for God's glory, they work for their own. Their output is impressive—a massive tower that reaches up to the heavens. But it's an expression of pride.

We glorify God when we give Him thanks for his world rather than pursuing our own fame. We glorify God when we give credit to Him for what we achieve, rather than claiming the credit for ourselves. We glorify God when we receive this world as a gift entrusted to us, rather than a resource to be exploited.

But there's another important way in which we glorify God through our work: *through work we serve other people*. It's such a simple observation, but it should have a profound effect on the way we think about our jobs.

All work of any worth blesses other people. We think of some professions as the "caring professions" (teaching, health care, social work). For these roles, it's easy to see how they serve other people—children get taught things, people are cured, families are supported and helped through difficulties. But we mustn't think for a moment that they're the *only* people who serve others.

If you work in a factory making toilet paper, then you serve other people. You serve them by providing them with toilet paper. And we can all agree that's an important service! If you're an accountant, then you serve other people by ensuring businesses are run well. If you're a delivery driver, then you serve people by ensuring the things they want or need get to them. If you're in advertising, then you serve other people by informing of new or better products. There aren't many jobs in which you can't identify who is served by your role. (And if you can't think who's served by what you do, then maybe it's time to get a new job.) You may never meet the people you're serving. But you're still serving them.

One way of thinking about this is to ask: *If nobody did my job, what would happen?* Imagine a world without toilet paper!

This makes a big difference to the way we think about work and its value. Every day you go to work, think about the people you're serving. Your work has real worth and importance. It's a way of blessing other people.

Our culture values work in terms of wages and salaries. The higher the salary, the more worthwhile the job. As believers, we need to think counter-culturally, by assessing the value of jobs by the service they render to others. Would you rather live in a world without toilet paper or a world without adverts?

Jesus was once asked what He thought was the greatest commandment:

> "The most important one," answered Jesus, "is this: 'Hear, O Israel: The Lord our God, the Lord is one. Love the Lord your God with all your heart and with all your soul and with all your mind and with all your strength.' The second is this: 'Love your neighbour as yourself.' There is no commandment greater than these."
>
> **Mark 12 v 29-31**

We love God through our work by doing it for His glory, rather than our own fame. And we love our neighbour through our work when we see it as an opportunity to bless other people.

The teacher of the law who asked Jesus the question replies:

> "To love him with all your heart, with all your understanding and with all your strength, and to love your neighbour as yourself is more important than all burnt offerings and sacrifices."
>
> **Mark 12 v 33-34**

Jesus, we're told, saw this as a wise answer from someone who was not far from God's kingdom. Loving God and people is more important than formal worship. Indeed work can be an act of worship if it's done to bless other people and bring God glory. Paul says:

> I urge you, brothers and sisters, in view of God's mercy, to offer your bodies as a living sacrifice, holy and pleasing to God—this is your true and proper worship. **Romans 12 v 1**

The worship of God's people when we gather together is really important. It's an opportunity to remind one another that God is more precious than anything else. But it's not the only time we worship. The whole of life is an opportunity to worship God. Zechariah says that, in the kingdom of God, even the pots and pans are holy to God—as holy as the sacred bowls in the temple (Zechariah 14 v 20-21). Even washing up can be holy to the Lord. We can offer up our routine chores as a holy act, consecrated to God's glory.

Questions for reflection

- How does your work bless other people?

- What if your work is not blessing others? What should you do when your company makes decisions that you're not happy with as a Christian?

In Revelation 18 v 4, the apostle John calls on Christians to "come out" of Babylon—a symbol of the Roman system. Yet Daniel maintained his integrity while serving at the heart of the original Babylon (even when it meant risking death).

- When should we follow the call of John and when should we follow the example of Daniel?

- What difference does your proximity to the decisions make? Does it matter whether it's just your team, or the whole company that makes an unethical decision? What if your department blesses people, but another part of the company is behaving in an ungodly way?

11 DECISIONS

Principle

Link your decisions to a Christian worldview.

Consider this

Dave had been really challenged by Sunday's sermon. His pastor had told them that all of life was to be lived under the lordship of Christ. "Of course that's right," thought Dave. His pastor had encouraged them to think about how the gospel related to their decisions in the home, the workplace and church.

Dave had been particularly challenged by the part about the workplace. He wasn't sure he ever thought very much about Jesus at work. But today would be different. Today he would let Jesus be Lord of his work.

Now he sat at his desk with a proposal to buy new office chairs. "Jesus is Lord," he told himself. "Jesus is Lord of chairs?" Maybe this was going to be harder than he first thought. What has Jesus got to do with new chairs?

Biblical background

Read Colossians 1 v 15-20.

- What is the role of Jesus in creation?

- List what was covered by His work of creation?

- What is the implication of His role in creation according to verse 17?

- What is the scope of Jesus' work of redemption?

Read Luke 3 v 10-14; 19 v 8-10 and Acts 24 v 24-26.

- How do John, Jesus and Paul spell out in these stories what difference becoming a Christian should make to our actions and behaviour?

Read all about it

All of working life is spent making decisions. This is especially true of managers, but *everyone* has to make decisions in the workplace.

- *How should I respond to this customer?*
- *Does this plug require a 3-amp fuse or a 13-amp fuse?*
- *Which of these applicants should I hire?*

Would a Christian employee or boss think about these decisions differently from a non-Christian?

Some things that help teams work well are not distinctly Christian (like having clear goals, for example). Some good working qualities reflect Christian values (eg: good listening reflects a commitment to love other people), but they're hardly things that *only* Christians do. Where does Christian distinctiveness come into play?

We don't have to justify every action with a Bible verse. But we do have to ensure that all our actions are part of an approach to work that is shaped by a broad biblical framework. It can be helpful to think in terms of a ladder with different levels of application. The ladder is made up of the following categories:

Worldview
Values
Principles and Goals
Policies and Decisions
Practice

Each category is like the rung of a ladder that enables us to move down (putting our worldview into practice) or up (showing how our practice reflects our worldview). Our worldview shapes our values. Our values shape the principles and goals we adopt. These determine our policies and decisions, which are then implemented through our practice. The ladder shows how theological ideas are linked to practical action.

For example:

Worldview	People are made in God's image—and God said bodily existence is good.
Values	We value people and are concerned for their physical needs.
Principles and Goals	**Principle:** our working environment should be safe. **Goal:** we will create a safe working environment.

Policies and Decisions	**Policy:** we will provide a safe chair for every employee. **Decision:** we will replace our chairs with the "Super-Safe" model from Easy Chairs Ltd.
Practice	Purchase new chairs.

This model shows how our theology can be linked to our practice. Another manager may purchase the same model of chairs. So, in one sense, buying chairs is not a distinctly Christian action. Yet we can show how buying those chairs is informed by a biblical worldview. This gets us away from proof-texting. Not every decision requires biblical reflection when our lives and our work are rooted in a broader biblical framework.

Notice, too, that as we go down the ladder, Christian distinctiveness decreases. Isaiah says:

> When a farmer ploughs for planting, does he plough continually? Does he keep on breaking up and working the soil? When he has levelled the surface, does he not sow caraway and scatter cumin? Does he not plant wheat in its place, barley in its plot, and spelt in its field? His God instructs him and teaches him the right way. Caraway is not threshed with a sledge, nor is a cartwheel rolled over cumin; caraway is beaten out with a rod, and cumin with a stick. Grain must be ground to make bread; so one does not go on threshing it for ever. Though he drives the wheels of his threshing-cart over it, his horses do not grind it. All this also comes from the LORD Almighty, wonderful in counsel and magnificent in wisdom. **Isaiah 28 v 24-29**

There is a wisdom to work that reflects the way the world was made. And unbelievers sense this, even if they don't credit it to God. Their good working practices come from "the LORD Almighty, wonderful in counsel and magnificent in wisdom." Theologians call this "common grace". God graciously "instructs" both believers and unbelievers, and "teaches [them] the right way". So, at the bottom of the ladder, we can borrow freely from the wisdom of the world.

This model helps us decide whether we need specifically Christian input or not. We don't have to do biblical reflection on everything that moves! Not every decision requires biblical reflection. In this example, we don't need to go to Christians to find out which are the best chairs. Yet our actions are still biblically informed.

A biblical worldview

To shape our actions by a Christian worldview, we need to think in terms of the Bible's big story. We should explore issues by looking at them in the light of creation, the fall, redemption (promised in the Old Testament and accomplished through Jesus) and the hope of a new creation.

For any issue we can ask ourselves:

- In relation to this issue, how does the way God made the world express His character and will? How is this revealed in the Bible?
- How does sin affect this issue? How do I need to take into account human selfishness?
- How does the Old Testament reveal God's character and will?
- How does the Old Testament increase our understanding of what Jesus has done for us and the example He sets us?
- How do the teachings and example of Jesus and the apostles relate to this issue?
- How does our new identity in Christ and membership of His new community affect our approach to this issue?
- What does the pattern of the cross mean for this issue?
- How does our hope of a renewed creation inform our approach to this issue?
- How does the fact that full redemption is in the future qualify present perspectives on this issue?

Questions for reflection

Think about a decision that is facing you at work. Or an imaginary case, like someone responding to an angry customer, or a manager deciding whether to offer flexible working hours.

- Identify for this decision what each of the different rungs of the ladder linking theology to practice might look like:
  - Worldview
  - Values
  - Principles and goals
  - Policies and decisions
  - Practice

- Identify how each of the main stages of the Bible story might shape a theology relevant to this decision:
  - Creation
  - Fall
  - Redemption
  - New creation

12 WITNESS

Principle

Embrace the unique opportunities for witness at work with courage, patience and integrity.

Consider this

"Craig's asked me to get involved in the youth group," said Colleen. "And I'd like to help. But I can't be sure of getting back from work in time. And besides, I'm pretty done in by Friday evenings. I'm not sure how I'd cope with 20 teenagers!"

"I'm sure you'd be great with them," said Pete, her pastor. "But if it's not going to work for you, that's fine."

"Are you sure?"

"Yes, of course." Pete could see something was wrong. "You alright?"

"I feel so guilty about not doing any evangelism. I mean, I love Jesus and I want others to know about Him. But work takes up so much of my time. I've been wondering whether I should look for a less demanding job."

"Maybe," said Pete. "That's a good option. But what about your current job? Doesn't that give you opportunities?"

"I'm not sure that really counts. None of my colleagues lives close to the church, so I can't really invite them along."

"Hmm, that doesn't help," said Peter. "But..."

Biblical background

Read 1 Peter 2 v 9 – 3 v 7

- How does Peter describe Christians in verses 9-10?
- What evangelistic strategy does he commend in 2 v 12?
- How does this apply in the workplace (2 v 18-21) and home (3 v 1-7)?
- How are we to respond to hostility?
- How does the call to abstain from sinful desires in 2 v 11 apply in your workplace?
- What evangelistic strategy does he commend in 3 v 15-16?

Read all about it

What do you think of when you think about evangelism? The Alpha Course? Christianity Explored? Guest services? Street preaching? Door-to-door visitation?

We often think of evangelism in terms of *events*. Nothing wrong with that. It's really important that churches give opportunities for unbelievers to hear the gospel explained. But evangelism is bigger than evangelistic events. Much bigger.

Jesus didn't just send the Holy Spirit so we could *do* evangelism. He gave us the Spirit so we could *be* witnesses—so our whole lives would commend the good news about Jesus. Peter says:

> Live such good lives among the pagans that, though they accuse you of doing wrong, they may see your good deeds and glorify God on the day he visits us. **1 Peter 2 v 12**

And Peter expands on this, not by describing evangelistic events, but by talking about the witness of Christians in the wider world (2 v 13-17), in the workplace (2 v 18-25) and in the home (3 v 1-7). Our whole lives are to be evangelistic events!

You in your workplace

The workplace is a great context for Christian witness. Churches often spend time thinking about how they can build relationships with unbelievers, when, all the time, those relationships already exist at work. We often share our lives in the workplace with people who would never dream of attending a church. We may be their only contact with the gospel. People can avoid most forms of evangelism. They can throw away a gospel tract or close the door to the person who knocks on the door. But they can't avoid the witness of a Christian colleague.

The church in Philippi might have wondered whether God was really in control of the mission of His church. The church's best missionary had been imprisoned. No more synagogue debates. No more public lectures. No more open-air preaching. But Paul was excited by the opportunities his imprisonment had given him.

Twenty-four hours a day, he was chained to a guard. One by one, they would have taken it in turns to sit with him, with nothing to do except talk to the great evangelist! So Paul says:

> Now I want you to know, brothers and sisters, that what has happened to me has actually served to advance the gospel. As a result, it has become clear throughout the whole palace guard and to everyone else that I am in chains for Christ. **Philippians 1 v 12-13**

Living the gospel

The attitudes of Christians to their work, and their conduct at work, have huge potential to commend the gospel to others:

> Make it your ambition to lead a quiet life: you should mind your own business and work with your hands, just as we told you, so that your daily life may win the respect of outsiders and so that you will not be dependent on anybody. **1 Thessalonians 4 v 11-12**

> Teach slaves to be subject to their masters in everything, to try to please them, not to talk back to them, and not to steal from them, but to show that they can be fully trusted, so that in every way they will make the teaching about God our Saviour attractive. **Titus 2 v 9-10**

Our attitude to authority, the way we treat colleagues and clients, our punctuality, our kindness (especially to those below us in the hierarchy), our conscientiousness and our integrity—all will commend our Saviour. Often we don't see much change and we can think we're not making much difference. But our impact on people can be profound. Listen to the words of a friend of mine:

> We need to recognise the profoundness of work relationships. What do I mean? Colleagues who know each other for a while see each other in extreme situations. My colleagues are far more likely to see me in a high-stress situation than my family, friends or contacts out of work. And I see them in those situations too. This can be an emotionally charged shared experience. It must create opportunities for real friendship and gospel opportunity. Work relationships have a

distance between them which is right and proper. Yet colleagues see deep things about each other.

Sharing the gospel

Lives that commend the gospel are not enough. We need to be ready to give an answer for the hope that we have (1 Peter 3 v 15). If we never explain the gospel, then people will probably assume we live a good life so we can earn our way into heaven. Or they'll give us the credit. They'll think of us as good people, rather than people who know a great Saviour. So we need to tell people the message of Jesus and what He's done for us through His death and resurrection.

Your context will affect your approach:

- If you're visiting another site or a contractor or working in a place with high staff turn-over, then you'll need to be bold because you may only have one or two opportunities with people.
- If you're likely to be working with the same people for months or years, or if you're junior in the hierarchy, then you may need to be patient and pray that your life will create good opportunities.
- In some professions, employees are concerned about you using your position to share the gospel with clients, but you can still find opportunities with your colleagues.

Another challenge with sharing the gospel in the workplace is this. We think the message of Jesus is exciting good news. But it can feel as if many of the opportunities thrown up in the workplace push us into talking about bad news. We can end up looking like joyless prudes who want to stamp out people's fun.

Consider the following comments from Christian workers:

"What responsibility do I have to be the 'morality police', chastising people for swearing or looking at dodgy emails?"

> "Conversations often get quite obscene. I find it hard to know how to handle these—to be people's friends without getting drawn into that."

> "People get onto dirty jokes, sexist comments, assumptions of dishonesty or impropriety very early in a relationship at work. And if you don't play along, you'll have to do so publicly."

There are no simple answers to any of these challenges. But one approach is to think in terms of saying "needn't", rather than "shouldn't". "Shouldn't" is the language of legalism and legalism is never good news. But the gospel not only tells what we should and shouldn't do, it also gives us the motives and resources to live the good life. It offers us a bigger and better life than the false promises of sin. So we can say more than "I shouldn't lie at work". We can say: "I needn't lie at work, because I have a Father in heaven who cares for me" or "I don't need to prove myself, because I have God's approval in Christ".

You might not feel that you can explain the gospel very well to people or answer all their questions. This is where events like guest services and evangelistic courses come into their own. You can invite someone to an event, like Levi who invited his friends to eat with Jesus (Luke 5 v 27-32). Or you might want to consider getting involved in work-based opportunities, like lunchtime Bible studies or after-work events.

The guards who sat next to Paul in prison were brought into contact with the gospel message through their working lives. Think about the people you sit next to. Or the people you travel with. You have a job to do, so clearly you can't spend all your time talking about Jesus as Paul could do in prison. But working life throws up lots of opportunities for conversations. You can talk while you're doing manual work, or during shared journeys or lunch breaks, or over a drink after work.

Ideas for action

1. Here are some tips for workplace witness.
   Which ones could you apply in your situation?

   - Let everyone know you're a Christian as soon as possible in a new work situation.

   - Take a genuine interest in people and their families.

   - Lasting workplace friendships nearly always have a life outside the workplace itself, so look for opportunities to spend time with people outside of work.

   - Pray for your colleagues by name. Pray that the Holy Spirit would create opportunities for you to talk about Jesus—and give you the boldness to grab them.

   - Get involved in lunchtime Bible studies or after-work events.

2. Have a good answer ready for the Monday-morning question: *What did you get up to this weekend?* Try to think of something a bit more intriguing than simply: *I went to church.* Talk about how you saw God at work or what you discovered in the sermon.

   - Think about last weekend. What answer could you have had ready for the question: "What did you do this weekend?"

13 COMMUNITY

Principle

Find opportunities to encourage Christians in the workplace.

Consider this

Irene was about to go off to teach science to missionary children in a mission school in Africa. She was standing at the front of church while her pastor interviewed her, before he laid hands on her and prayed for her.

Sandra sat in a pew next to her friend Jane. "Jane teaches science, too," she thought. "And in a challenging inner-city school. Every day her work means she has contact with children from broken families. She's making a big difference in many of their lives, even though it's really tough going."

Sandra was delighted that Irene was leaving her homeland to serve Christ as a missionary and she knew it was going to be hard for her, living away from her family. But she started to wonder why Jane had never stood at the front with people laying hands on her. "I reckon," she thought to herself, "that her work at the school is just as as big and hard a mission field. Maybe more so."

Biblical background
Read Ephesians 4 v 7-16

- Does verse 14 ever describe your life at work?

- How do we help one another become mature Christians in the workplace?

- What gifts has God given Christians you know that could help you live as a Christian at work?

- What gifts has God given you that could help other Christian workers?

Read all about it

We're not meant to live the Christian life on our own.

We're made in the image of the trinitarian God to live in relationship. Our sin means those relationships are now often marked by conflict or fragmentation. But we still work best when we work together. And Christ died for His bride, the church (Ephesians 5 v 25-27). He died to create a people who would be God's people. The cross reconciles us to God and to one another (Ephesians 2 v 14-18).

The church is the community where we belong to one another, with all the responsibility that ownership implies (see Romans 12 v 5). God gave us the Christian community so that we might grow together to appreciate Christ's love and grow together to maturity in

Him (Ephesians 3 v 18; 4 v 11-16).

Yet the workplace can be a lonely place for Christians. You may be the only believer in your team or your division or even your company. And the workplace can be a hostile environment for Christians. You may be the butt of jokes. Or you may experience direct, aggressive opposition to your face and behind your back. Things only get worse when you try to live in a way shaped by your faith or speak up for Jesus. Your behaviour may well be a challenge to other people. You may not personally confront people, but your integrity exposes their lack of integrity. It can be a tough place to live as a Christian.

So look for support.

Christians in your workplace

If there are other Christians in your workplace, then be explicit about supporting one another. That could involve:

- an occasional conversation about the pressures you share;
- regularly praying together for your integrity and opportunities to witness to Christ;
- joining one another when you go for a drink after work so you can support one another in conversations about Jesus;
- a lunchtime Bible study or evangelistic events.

It's very easy to keep your head down when you're on your own. But when there are two of you, you can hold one another accountable and work together to witness to Christ.

Christians in your profession

Each profession throws up its own dilemmas for believers. It might be the challenge of medical ethics for those in health care. It might be ethical practices for those in multinational corporations. It might be the challenge of coarse joking or aggressive behaviour for those in manual jobs.

For some professions, there are Christian associations that offer a lot of help in thinking through your work from a biblical perspective. For others, you might find it helpful to talk through the issues with other people in your local church in the same kind of role, as well as then holding one another accountable.

Christians in your church

Because, for most people, their working life takes place outside the neighbourhood of their local church, it often goes unnoticed and unrecognized. Yet work is where most Christians:

- spend most of their lives;
- face their biggest challenges;
- get their best opportunities to point others to Christ.

So it's important for churches to celebrate the world of work and to look for opportunities to support people in the pressures that work brings. This commitment to work should be reflected in our mission strategies, our expectations for workers, our application of the Bible, our prayers, the people we interview in meetings, what we celebrate and how we illustrate our sermons.

Opportunities to follow up witness in work often take place off-site and out of work-hours. You may get a chance to say something in a coffee or tea break, but the chance to talk in greater depth is more likely to come when you have lunch or a drink at the pub after work. That means that churches need to recognise and value these opportunities, even if it means people cannot get to evening church activities.

Spontaneity can be difficult for workers, especially if they have a significant commute after work. It's hard to be positive when someone who's not had a long day at work calls you at 7.30pm suggesting an activity for that evening. It's often easier to manage time and energy with pre-planned activities.

Churches can sometimes express appreciation for the so-called caring professions, but be wary of business people, because they spend their time dealing with money. But we need a church culture in which business is affirmed and entrepreneurs are encouraged, because business blesses our world by creating employment, providing services, generating tax revenue and resourcing mission. Business people interested in Jesus should feel welcome and affirmed.

Money can also be idolatrous, a rival to God for our affections and a threat to our relationships. So Christian business people need to be accountable for the way they generate wealth and the use to which they put it. We want people to be generous, avoiding excessive expenditure. But we shouldn't warn against those dangers in a way that portrays business negatively, nor affirm the service professions in a way that business people find excluding.

Questions for reflection

- What opportunities are there for you to co-operate with:
  - Christians in your workplace?
  - Christians in your profession?
  - Christians in your church?
- What opportunities could you create?

Ideas for action

Supporting Christian workers in the church

Here are some ideas for ways in which churches can support Christian workers. Which is your church already doing? Which could you start to do?

- Think whether any of the times of your meetings could work better for workers who commute. Shorter meetings might work well early in the evening, so people can attend on the way home from work. Otherwise, you need to allow time for people to get home, prepare a meal, put children to bed and so on, before expecting them to be out in the evening.
- Make church business meetings relaxed and informal, so they don't feel like a burden or another work meeting.
- Visit people in their workplace to see where they work, meet their colleagues and pray for them in context.
- "Commission" people who are embarking on new jobs or new roles, just as we commission people beginning new pastoral roles or missionary service.
- Have a regular "window on the workplace" when you gather as a church, in which someone talks about their work and shares prayer needs.
- Send a regular email to workers in their workplace with a brief "thought for the day".
- Routinely include application to the workplace in sermons and Bible studies. ("How would this passage apply in the office or workshop when someone says…?")

Supporting Christian entrepreneurs

Many of today's big companies were originally started by Christians with support from their local church. How could you support business people and entrepreneurs in your congregation? Here are some ideas.

- A mentoring scheme linking new entrepreneurs with experienced business people, to help develop business plans, access resources, generate ideas and solve issues.
- A business club, so business people can meet for peer support and accountability, and to link investors with missional business opportunities.
- A skills bank, providing free or low-cost start-up support (accountancy, business advice, design) plus a database of government and other resources for new businesses.
- Training in the vision and practice of missional business.

CONCLUSION

14 TAKING GOD TO WORK

Principle

Expect God to be at work—at work.

Consider this

Maggie looked up from her computer screen. She'd overheard Doug and Colin talking—something about church. It didn't take long to work out they were talking about how Christians hate gays.

"No," she wanted to say. "It's more complicated than that."

She knew it was something to do with orientation and lifestyle. Was that right? She tried to remember the talk at church a few months ago. It was complicated. Too complicated for her to explain.

And she didn't want to look like a bigot. "Better to keep quiet on this one," she said to herself. "I'm having enough trouble trying to make this spreadsheet work."

Biblical background

Read Genesis 39

- What were Joseph's working conditions like?

- How did Joseph behave under pressure?

- What was the secret of Joseph's success?

Read all about it

A survey by the London Institute for Contemporary Christianity (LICC) asked Christians what were the main problems they faced at work. The top answers were:

- stress and burnout
- maintaining Christian integrity
- communications and relationships
- overwork and long-hours
- insecurity and redundancy/lay-offs

It can be tough! In many other contexts you can shape the culture. But at work you inhabit an existing culture, a culture that is potentially hostile to Jesus and in which you may be in a minority of one.

Many years before Jesus, a raiding party of Arameans captured a young Israelite girl. She found herself working as a slave for Naaman, the commander of the Aramean army. She was alone in a hostile country, without rights, working for God's enemies. And yet God used her in an amazing way.

Naaman became ill with leprosy. She could have kept silent to avoid trouble. She could have rejoiced in the misfortune that had befallen her master. Instead:

> She said to her mistress, "If only my master would see the prophet who is in Samaria! He would cure him of his leprosy." **2 Kings 5 v 3**

Surprisingly, Naaman listened to her advice, and was (eventually) cured of leprosy and became a follower of the living God.

Work can be a hostile place for Christians. But it can also be a place of amazing opportunity.

Trusting God at work

That same LICC survey found that the greatest temptation Christians face at work is *self-reliance*.

Like the young Israelite girl in Naaman's household, Joseph was a slave with no rights, away from the community of faith in a hostile situation. But Genesis 39 v 2 tells us that "the LORD was with Joseph and he prospered" while he worked in Potiphar's house (Genesis 39v2). It goes on:

> When his master saw that the LORD was with him and that the LORD gave him success in everything he did, Joseph found favour in his eyes and became his attendant. Potiphar put him in charge of his household, and he entrusted to his care everything he owned.
>
> **Genesis 39 v 3-4**

It was the Lord's presence with Joseph that enabled him to maintain his integrity, when faced with temptation from Potiphar's wife.

Falsely accused, Joseph found himself in prison. But again we read:

> But while Joseph was there in the prison, the LORD was with him; he showed him kindness and granted him favour in the eyes of the prison warden. So the warden put Joseph in charge of all those held in the prison, and he was made responsible for all that was done there. **Genesis 39 v 20-22**

Joseph prospered at work because the Lord was with him. That didn't mean everything was straightforward for him—after all, he did end up in prison. But the knowledge of God's presence and blessing enables him to keep his integrity and to fulfil his work well. God continued to be with Joseph and prospered his work. Eventually, Joseph became "prime minister" in Egypt, which enables him to save many people from famine. More than that, God used Joseph's work to preserve His people and the promise they carried of a Redeemer.

Work brings many opportunities and many challenges. On our own, they are too much for us. But we're not on our own. Christians in the workplace are never alone. We have God's Spirit within us to empower us to live for Christ. When we rely on ourselves, things go wrong. On a good day we'll be filled with pride. On a bad day we'll find we can't cope and we succumb to temptation. So we need to cultivate a strong sense of reliance on God in the workplace.

There's an annual "take your daughter to work" day. The aim is for girls to experience the world of work and break down prejudices about women's roles. What about a "take your God to work" day? What difference would it make if you thought about taking God to work with you each day? What difference would it make if you thought of Jesus standing beside you in difficult moments? What difference would it make if you thought of the Holy Spirit living in you when gospel opportunities arise? Jesus said:

> "All authority in heaven and on earth has been given to me. Therefore go and make disciples of all nations, baptising them in the name of the Father and of the Son and of the Holy Spirit, and teaching them

to obey everything I have commanded you. *And surely I am with you always, to the very end of the age.*" **Matthew 28 v 18-20**

In your workplace, the Father watches over you, the Son stands beside you and the Spirit lives within you. God is at work—at work.

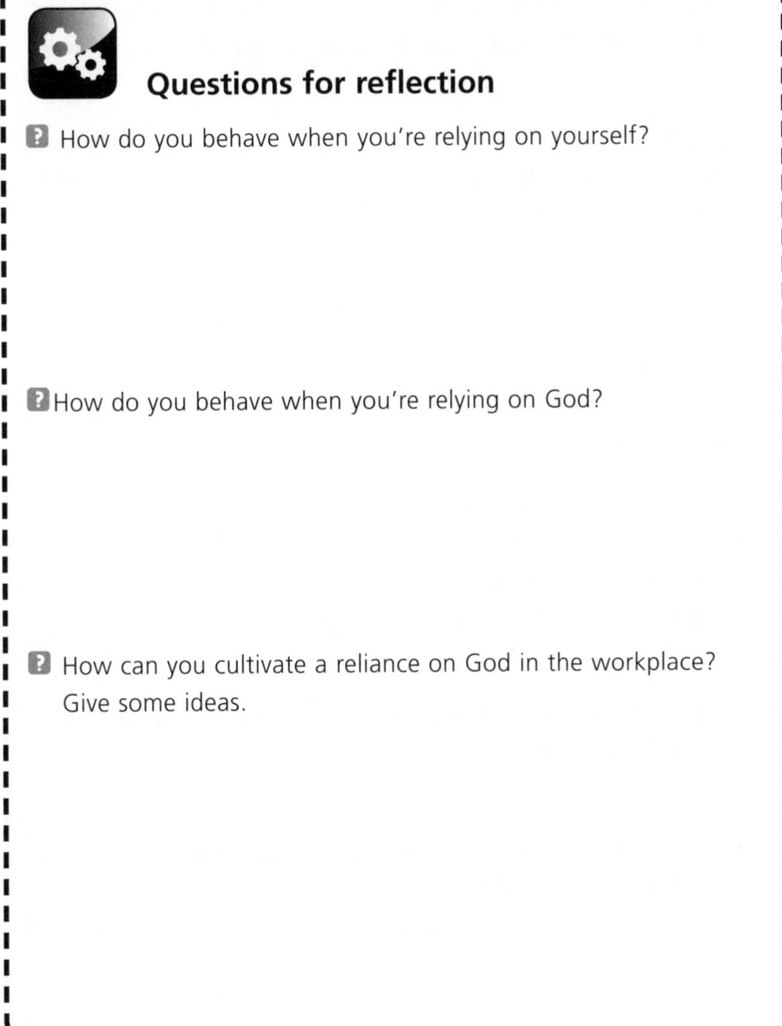

Questions for reflection

- How do you behave when you're relying on yourself?

- How do you behave when you're relying on God?

- How can you cultivate a reliance on God in the workplace? Give some ideas.

Ideas for action

- When you read the Bible, ask God to speak to you through His Spirit. Ask Him to show you how the passage speaks to the challenges you face in your workplace. Ask Him to show you how you could share what you're reading with a colleague.

- Bring work problems to God in prayer—both the specific challenges you face as a Christian and the work problems faced by you or your team.

- Pray for your colleagues and tell them you're praying for them.

- Pray through Bible passages, so that you turn what the Bible says into prayer.

- Put a verse up on your desk or in your tool box or on your screen-saver or on your dashboard—something to remind you of Christ's work for you, or the Spirit's work in you.

- Pray that the Holy Spirit would give you boldness. Adapt the prayer of Acts 4 v 23-31.

- Put yourself in situations where you know you will feel out of your comfort zone so you're forced to rely on God. Perhaps you could share your faith with your boss or ask colleagues how you can pray for them?

FURTHER READING

- Mark Greene, *Thank God It's Monday: Ministry in the Workplace*, Scripture Union
- Tim Keller, *Every Good Endeavour: Connecting Your Work to God's Plan for the World*, Hodder & Stoughton
- Tim Chester, *Work Songs*, A Good Book Guide, The Good Book Company
- Tim Chester, *The Busy Christians Guide to Busyness*, IVP

Gospel-centred marriage

becoming the couple God wants you to be

To understand why marriages struggle—as they all do—we need to understand the nature of our sin. To make marriages work, we need to understand how to apply the truth about God and His salvation. This study guide on Christian marriage focuses on how the gospel shapes the practical realities of everyday life. Tim Chester lifts the lid on many of the common pressure points, and shows how a proper understanding of the gospel can shape a response.

Gospel-centred family

becoming the parents God wants you to be

Many books aim to raise up competent, balanced parents and well-trained, well-rounded children. But Tim Chester and Ed Moll focus on families growing God-knowing, Christ-confessing, grace-receiving, servant-hearted, mission-minded believers—adults and children together. In twelve concise chapters, this book challenges us to become the distinctively different people that God, through His gospel, calls us to be.

Gospel-centred church

becoming the community God wants you to be

In *Gospel-centred church*, Steve Timmis and Tim Chester explain that gospel ministry is much more than simply evangelism. It is about shaping the whole of our church life and activities by the content and imperatives of the gospel. It is about ensuring that our church or group is motivated by and focused on the gospel, as opposed to our traditions. This workbook is designed to help clarify our thinking about how we should live our lives as the people of God.

Gospel-centred life

becoming the person God wants you to be

How can ordinary Christians live the truly extraordinary life that God calls us to? By focusing our attention on the grace of God shown to us in the gospel, everyday problems familiar to Christians everywhere can be transformed as the cross of Christ becomes the motive and measure of everything we do. *Gospel-centred life* shows how every Christian can follow the way of the cross, as they embrace the liberating grace of God.

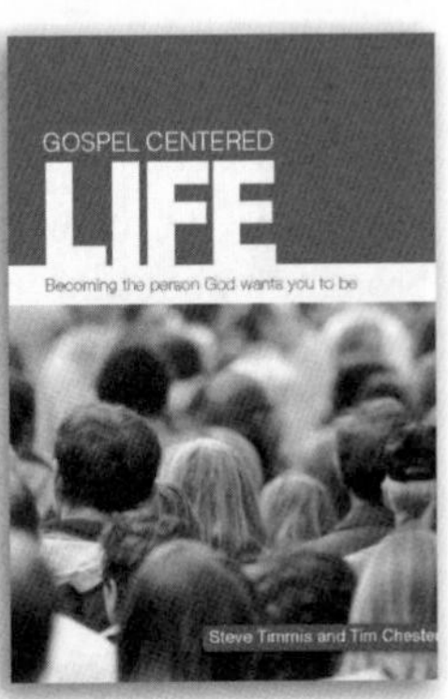

Delighting in the Trinity

Why Father, Son and Spirit are such good news

The Trinity is at the heart of all that Christians believe. And rather than be a source of embarrassment, properly understood, it should fill us with joy. This book aims to help you see how the Trinity is fantastically good news. God sent His Son and His Spirit into our world to draw us into a wonderful relationship with Himself. This is the God who gives meaning and joy to our lives.

From creation to new creation

Making sense of the whole Bible story

Sometimes it's hard to see the wood for the trees. Running through the many gripping and memorable stories the Bible contains is one big story of God's plan for the world He made, and how He brought it about through Jesus Christ. Packed with diagrams, illustrations and timelines, this accessible Bible overview unlocks the storyline of the whole Bible—how God promised and then brought about the plan to save our fallen world. It is a story that will encourage effective, active Christian living in today's world.

Work Songs

Exploring frustration, compromise, stress and joy from the Psalms

Six studies looking at six psalms to "sing" in the workplace. For many Christians there is a gap between church on Sunday and work on Monday. These songs encourage us to bridge that gap. Great for workers everywhere and ideal for working through in twos or threes as well as in larger groups.

Living in the real world

The Good Book Guide to 1 Peter

Wise Christians understand that opposition and suffering are normal for the church and are prepared for anything. That's why Christians today need the message of 1 Peter—a letter to first-century believers surrounded by trials and hostility. Why does God let this happen? How can my faith survive? How should I treat those who cause me suffering? These questions and more are covered in five sessions full of practical application. Let's be prepared, so that our faith "may be proved genuine and may result in praise, glory and honour when Jesus Christ is revealed".

At The Good Book Company, we are dedicated to helping Christians and local churches grow. We believe that God's growth process always starts with hearing clearly what He has said to us through His timeless word—the Bible.

Ever since we opened our doors in 1991, we have been striving to produce resources that honour God in the way the Bible is used. We have grown to become an international provider of user-friendly resources to the Christian community, with believers of all backgrounds and denominations using our Bible studies, books, evangelistic resources, DVD-based courses and training events.

We want to equip ordinary Christians to live for Christ day by day, and churches to grow in their knowledge of God, their love for one another, and the effectiveness of their outreach.

Call us for a discussion of your needs or visit one of our local websites for more information on the resources and services we provide.

UK & Europe: www.thegoodbook.co.uk
North America: www.thegoodbook.com
Australia: www.thegoodbook.com.au
New Zealand: www.thegoodbook.co.nz

UK & Europe: 0333 123 0880
North America: 866 244 2165
Australia: (02) 6100 4211
New Zealand (+64) 3 343 1990